TOM AL...

by

Bill Shannon

Contents

Handsel 'Nutshell' Booklet no. 5

British Library Cataloguing in Publication Data:
A catalogue record for this publication
is available from the British Library

ISBN   1 871828 53 8

Typeset in 10.5 pt. Garamond

Printed by Polestar Scientifica AUP, Aberdeen

Thanks are expressed to the Drummond Trust of 3 Pitt Terrace, Stirling,
to Mrs Jean Allan and to all who have encouraged the publication of this book

1 The Making of the Man

Easter morning in Reims, 1945. An ordinary service of worship organised by the US Army base. Of course there was nothing ordinary for anybody in Europe at that time. It was towards the end of the War. Everybody knew that a period of hell on earth was ending raising urgent questions for the future.

Tom Allan was there unexpectedly, on invitation by a friend, an American officer. He brought with him all 29 years of his life, specially focused by this historic time and urgently questioned by the 'What now?' of the future. Somewhere in the context of the worship that Easter day a black American GI rose to sing 'Were you there when they crucified my Lord?' It was a life changing moment for Tom Allan which he describes:

Now I had heard that sung hundreds of times. Indeed I'd sung it myself. But on that day in Reims as the soldier was singing, I realised for the first time – really for the first time – not as a theory, but on the pulses of my life, what the cross was about and what the Christian faith was about.

I realised for the first time that day that Christ had died for me. 'Were you there...?' How could I be there? This happened two thousand years ago. But the man who first sang those words had gone right to the heart of Christian truth and had in this simple spiritual, reminded us of the fact that we're all involved in the death of Christ.

And I remember thinking that, if my hand had helped to crucify him, then also I was there when he prayed 'Father, forgive them.' I was involved in Calvary and I was involved also in the forgiveness of God through Christ. That day, I heard unmistakeably speaking to me, the voice of God.

He was gripped by the thought, this is the true meaning of the Cross. It is not something that happened 2000 years ago, but something contemporary – and we are there. The intensely personal nature of the Christian belief about the death of Christ burned into his heart. It took weeks of wrestling in his own soul to confirm forever that in this experience God had called and he would obey. There is no understanding of the man without Easter Day in Rheims.

But Tom never underestimated the way by which he had come. Born of Ayrshire stock, his father was a butcher in the Irvine valley town of Newmilns, and Tom, the youngest of a family of eight, used many a 'crack' in pulpit and conversation which revealed his debt to the rich Ayrshire humour of the Robert Burns tradition. Here it was that he developed his lifelong interest in poetry and literature. He often said that poets and novelists have the keenest insight into modern life. The Valley Towns shared a legendary love of music – brass bands, male voice choirs and music festivals. Tom was an active participant from earliest years. He played both violin and piano 'in private' and with his light baritone voice he loved to sing the well-known duet from Bizet's 'The

Pearl Fishers' along with Archie Porterfield, Clerk to the Congregational Board in his first church. The people loved it, and the non-stop patter with it.

Tom gratefully acknowledged the role of his local village church. As a teenager, his brilliant searching mind, leadership skills and sporting prowess were all burgeoning into bloom. He was fortunate that the Revd Dr Bill Fitch arrived as the new minister. Only six years his senior, Bill Fitch soon valued highly his friendship with such a promising student. They met just after Tom's life had been dealt a shattering blow: without a moment's warning, his father died of a massive heart attack. Bill Fitch notes two significant effects of this for Tom. On the one hand it brought his faith to a more mature level, coping now with the shortness and uncertainty of life by lighting it up with assurance of eternal life. On the other hand the experience encouraged a premonition that he would die young. It was a powerful force which Tom would carry all his years, often quoting, 'As long as it is day, we must keep on doing the work of him who sent me; night is coming when no one can work.' Yet characteristically this potentially negative force was a spur to spend and be spent in service.

These years achieved the groundwork for Tom's future. Studies were always a thrill and a privilege, never a chore, and he crowned them with first class honours in English at Glasgow University. But such erudition, achieved without difficulty, was never esoteric. The comment of his first session clerk reveals all: 'Nane o' they scholar ministers for us, Mr Allan, just an ordinary man like yersel'.'

It is typical of the man that he combined this eminence in studies with the distinction of being a popular billiards champion of the University Union in 1939, much to his mother's disgust – but in his case no sign of misspent youth.

Tom was never stuck in his study with his books. He was involved with the people in the community and church life where he lived. Alongside his peers in Bible Class and youth work, he was a leader. He shared with Bill Fitch the work of Seaside Mission in Millport. His insight into the potential of such work was applied in all his future years, often against the stream.

We must speak about his mother and his home, because he often did. It was clear from the warmth of his shared memories that it was a happy home and a Christian one. His mother was a saint in Tom's eyes. He knew that her steadfast simple faith and her ceaseless prayers were of the very rock foundation of his life. As he said to a friend in the RAF, 'Two women are my ideals of womanhood – my mother and my wife.' His wife to be was Jean Dunn. She and Tom shared the same Irvine Valley homeland, the same school and the same church and youth fellowship. The chemistry that brought them to marriage was a powerful mix of mutual love and admiration, common background, shared interests and gifts, like music, united standards and aspirations about home and family life, and, above all, their Christian faith – independently held yet willingly shared. It was a relationship yet to be tested.

2

They were married in June 1941. The War was an immediate accessory to that testing and the eighteen demanding years of ministry which followed took it to the very limits. It was never found wanting.

The War found Tom Allan, already a divinity student, destined for the ministry of the Church. Although such students could be exempt from national service he left his studies and volunteered for the Royal Air Force. 'I am not sure whether it was a desire to be identified with the men or a desire to escape', he explained. There is no doubt that it was both. There is ample testimony from his many friends in the forces that 'he was good to be with'. One friend, a Canadian Scot, helps us to understand how much it was 'an escape' as well. Away from the influences of university, home and church, the growing questions and doubts raised by his wide studies, the awesome evils of war and the stark reality that few of his fellow servicemen shared the faith, all shook his foundations. He was led to a state of agnosticism, intellectual and moral breakdown, unbelief and disillusionment. It didn't help his morale that he had been 'grounded' from aircrew because of eyesight problems. A cruel blow to any flyer, but especially difficult for one who took such a pride in physical and mental fitness.

Nevertheless Tom Allan's record in the RAF is impressive. He joined as an A/c in the ranks, was given increasing responsibility over three years and then commissioned in the RAF Intelligence Service. He was finally posted to Supreme Headquarters. In spite of this successful wartime career, faced with specialist knowledge of war's worst atrocities, the remnant of schoolboy and student faith crumpled and Christian lifestyle faltered. Then - it was Easter.

The chapter of rural Ayrshire, student success, achievement and wartime melt-down was to end by the forging of the new man – 'ransomed, healed, restored, forgiven' – the new man 'in Christ' as described by the apostle Paul.

Emerging from Easter at Reims left the sphere of God's call on his life still to be interpreted. Should it be politics? The socialist ideals of the 'left' had always inspired him and, post war, he saw that they were urgent and possible for the people. His calling clarified for the ordained ministry, but that ministry always carried with it, as a simple assumption, that God cared about the total welfare of the people. Any genuine relationship with God was seen automatically to plunge you into the arena of 'quality of life' shared with your neighbour. There was never any question of driving a dividing wedge between 'the spiritual' and 'the material' or attempting to split the fundamental atom of faith, 'love God and love your neighbour.'

Tom Allan hurried home to family, church and university. He completed a hectic year taking the medal in New Testament studies combined with practical participation in D.P. Thomson's mission in Melrose Presbytery. Now the man was ready for the ministry.

2 The Man for the Ministry

In his book *The Face of my Parish* Tom Allan writes of his first impressions. 'I can still remember with great vividness the terror that took hold of me the first time I walked round my parish in September 1946. It seemed as if there was not love, but hostility, between us. I felt that all the windows were eyes looking into my soul and seeing the emptiness there. Where did one begin in such a situation? It was not long before the problems became articulate and well defined – and completely overwhelming.'

That initial uneasy relationship was shattered by meeting the people and quickly replaced by a mutual relationship only adequately expressed by the warm words of passionate love and unlimited devotion and sacrifice.

Nevertheless we will not understand the real Tom Allan if we miss the genuine honesty about himself and the refusal to hold any illusions about the situation facing the Christian ministry illustrated clearly in this typical parish.

He felt isolated by his culture, theology and even the 'dog-collar' and driven to despair by the communication gap between the Christian faith, fanned into flame for him by Easter at Reims, and the stolid indifference evident in the parish which treated the Church and the Faith as irrelevant.

This realistic analysis was not reversed in his thinking by the immediate success of his first year in North Kelvinside parish. The inspired preaching, the warm relationships, the pastoral care and the sheer hard work all lit up by the unique charisma with which God had endowed Tom Allan, had very measurable impact. A membership of 487 had grown to 611 in the first year and mainly from the parish. Tom Allan welcomed this response but judged it as but a scratch on the surface of a very hard problem.

The concept of the 'Missionary Parish' was basic to his ministry. The General Assembly of the Church of Scotland had just reasserted that assumption, but had noted the difficulty of making the system effective – especially in urban areas. Ministers were so over-stretched, serving the members, maintaining organisations, raising funds and fulfilling other public duties, that the major task of mission in the parish was ineffective or just left undone.

But this concept was facing criticism and challenge from two other sources. Some pointed to lifestyle changes claiming that 'urban parishes had ceased to be real communities and were more like Transit Camps'. Therefore meaningful contact and communication with people had moved from residence to workplace or leisure pursuits. An even more serious analysis was theological and struck, not at parish, but at the meaning of mission itself. Here the priority of the Church was not to convince people of the faith and so lead to new believers. Rather mission meant 'serving the people', seeking a just society. It was expressed as 'building the Kingdom of God' in the real world.

4

It is certainly to Tom Allan's credit that he found these criticisms with their hard lines of demarcation untenable, and he continued to see the parish as the place where they would be seen not to apply. Later, the city centre Parish of St George's-Tron would include the workplace, leisure activities and social challenges, as well as residence, all part of the parish responsibility.

A great step towards liberating the potential of the parish came with a bold experiment in Visitation Evangelism. Tom Allan pays tribute to D.P. Thomson, evangelist of the Church of Scotland who planned this effort. The novel factor of this visitation of nearly 2,000 homes was the recruitment of a team of volunteers from outside the parish itself, drawn from the personnel who had been engaged in the work of Seaside Mission under Mr Thomson's leadership. As well as students and a few ministers the 50 volunteers included many young men and women from business and industry. Their job was to pay a friendly visit, gather information, invite any with no Church connection to come to the parish church, and to witness to their faith appropriate to the situation. They found in 1947 hearts as well as doors open and welcoming.

A more tentative follow up team from the congregation, consisting of minister, assistants, Sunday School staff and some volunteer elders grew quickly in confidence and natural effectiveness as they realised that they too could serve the Church in this way.

Immediate results were dramatic. Nearly 100 new members joined, Sunday School doubled, every organisation increased with an accent on youth, and attendance at worship rose steadily. Also priorities clarified. 667 homes in the parish had no connection with any church. All the rest were either other Protestant Churches, Roman Catholic, or already belonged to the Parish Church.

Now the challenge was better defined if no less daunting. The information provided a basic picture on which future plans could be made. The good news was that a small nucleus of the congregation had caught the vision and were ready to serve in this newly discovered way. Their influence would inspire a much wider circle of faithful members of the congregation - vital for the future.

However many were indifferent and unwelcoming to any change. And of course, some were actively and verbally opposed. These forces, present in all congregations, were bound to cause problems.

News of this Visitation experiment spread widely and D.P. Thomson called on the Church to use it and adapt it to tackle the problem of the Parish. One very ambitious plan was the Glasgow Churches Campaign 1950. It was multi-faceted but the Congregational Committee, chaired by Tom Allan, concentrated on Visitation Evangelism. His own congregation, this time from its own resources, approached the job with enthusiasm. A second wave of response resulted and the dramatic statistic is that in five and a half years 800 new members joined the Church mainly from the busy area round its doors.

This brief summary brings us to the vital point. This mission success, not only numerical, but true and visible in people's faith and lifestyles, did not escape a far deeper analysis by Tom Allan. He noted that some, most of them men, came in expectantly ready to give of themselves for service to Christ, the Church and the Kingdom. Somehow they slid to the nominal edges of Church life or even away altogether. They found no place in Choirs, Sunday School staff, carpet bowls or holiday slides shows. What really had the Church to offer, assuming they survived the chill of unwelcoming long-term members?

He saw the Church trapped in its middle class culture, often forcing newcomers either to renounce their own 'class' or leave the Church with its alien class culture. Was there not a way of 'being the Church' which would save it from 'trivial pursuits' and leap these barriers?

Thus emerged the Congregational Group. Immediately after the first 'Parish Visitation' Tom Allan recognised that a small group of his members looked ready for serious business. Stretched beyond their normal pattern of church life, these folk had experienced a new dimension of commitment and were ready to develop it further. The more they caught the vision of a 'Missionary Parish' and tried to represent the Church and the Faith to their neighbours, the more they realised how poorly they were equipped for the job. They were not so much organised into a group as propelled into one by common needs.

Now this disparate, fully representative group began to gel as a genuine fellowship, shattering the image of urban church anonymity and mere nodding acquaintance. Soon there were rapid changes. The group was clearly too large for its functions. A pattern of house groups with lay leaders meeting three Wednesdays per month and coming together on the fourth was set up. This solved the hall accommodation problem and provided easy access for friends and neighbours. The Group doubled in size.

The need for a 'school of discipleship' became clear. Participants re-examined their Christian presuppositions, were inspired by the fellowship, and instead of wondering where they could serve Christ and his Church, now they could barely find the time to carry out a fraction of what was clearly needing done.

The implications for parish ministry priorities were vital. Freed from the tyranny of numbers, like members on the roll and pounds in the plate, ministers could focus on releasing the power latent in the highly committed minority and concentrate on enabling the Congregational Group to become a disciplined and trained spearhead for evangelism in the community. This new form of Parish Ministry would need courage to cope with the inevitable opposition to change and the demands that it would make on ministry.

Of course there were dangers. Separatist attitudes could cut the group off from the congregation; 'sincere misfits' could try to take over house groups; an inward looking group could easily forget the real world. The variety of group members in culture, class, intelligence, and most importantly, in spiritual capacity and awareness could stretch fellowship to breaking point. Tom Allan saw all these so clearly, yet would press on, as he saw lives changed, those sick and hurting in society healed, and the gap between church and parish being bridged. The inevitable tension, conflict and misunderstanding were to be expected, accepted and identified as marking the well sign-posted way of the Cross.

Could this shift in priorities, giving a central place to the Congregational Group, be contained within the accepted structure of the institutional Church? Certainly it could not, without radical change in that structure. Yet Emil Brunner's analysis concluded that without that sort of reformation it would be the institution that would die and the true *ecclesia* relocate.

A different critique suggests that the Congregational Group is a return to the 'gathered church' bringing together like-minded, 'committed' individuals into the welcoming warmth of a group of kindred spirits. This misconception is exploded by the actual evolution and effectiveness of the Congregational Group in North Kelvinside Parish. Clearly it became a living example of Archbishop Temple's classic description of the Church as the only society which does not exist for the benefit of its members but for service of others.

Over the next three years the statistics of this 'Missionary Parish' speak clearly enough. Membership increased to 1300; over 400 at morning service and nearly same again in the evening, helped by 100 visitors. Sunday Schools, Bible Class, Youth Fellowship, youth organisations and Woman's Guild were all booming. However the bare statistics are unable to convey the quiet, secret, long-term work that was being carried out in the parish, alongside neighbours, towards those attracted by the reputation of the North Kelvinside Church and not least among young people. Moreover, the quality and effectiveness of corporate Christian lifestyle in this Church and Parish had risen notably. At the centre of it all was the gifted and dedicated ministry of Tom Allan.

The Church of Scotland was finding ways of using these gifts more widely. Soon Tom was working with D.P. Thomson in Parish and Area missions and especially in the growing work of Seaside Missions in the summer. It was out of his leadership of Seaside Missions, supported by a keen group of able ministers and a growing core of committed lay people that United Christian Witness emerged. They organised monthly Evangelistic Rallies in North Kelvinside and helped with many parish missions during the winter, and staffed the Seaside Missions in the summer. They formed a strong support group for Tom Allan's extra parochial work for many years.

The impact of his ministry was widened even further by broadcasting. His 'Lift Up Your Hearts' series drew a flood of letters in response. Such interest needed nurturing and servicing by the Church. But parish ministers then had no secretarial help. All administration had to be done from home with no appropriate equipment to suit the job. It took years to establish this basic staff and office resource and not without personal costs in time and domestic readjustments for the Allans. What he saw clearly was another ministry emerging. People seeking, hurting and discovering would not come to Tom Allan and have to go away empty. Here too he would spend himself, backed by family and devoted helpers, to represent that Lord who had said, 'I will never turn away anyone who comes to me.'

Dr Ronald Falconer was in charge of BBC Religious broadcasting during 'the Golden Years of Radio' and into the beginnings of Television. In 1950 he was able to pioneer the first Radio Mission, a unique experiment in Radio Evangelism by a national broadcasting system. Naturally Tom Allan was one of the two dozen Radio Missioners selected to share in six weeks of special programmes in a great variety of formats. Tom's role was a vital one. An evening service from North Kelvinside on 1st October with five lay members sharing what church membership meant to them; a class of preparation for intending new members every Wednesday for six weeks broadcast from the studio; an evening service of membership for those joining after the preparation class. The two Sunday services fitted in to a normal pattern of broadcasting, albeit with fresh features. But the classes in the Christian Faith were different. This had not been done before. A letter came in rating Tom Allan's 'The way to live', 'the finest religious broadcasting I have ever heard.' One week a listener research report gave it appreciation index points higher than any other Scottish broadcast religious or secular.

Ronnie Falconer wrote, 'This was uncompromising Christian broadcasting which went out on a weeknight in the middle of entertainment; solid Christian teaching with question and answer thereon.' Clearly radio was releasing the spiritual gifts of the evangelist to be effective far beyond the parish. But the parishes were not yet alert to it. Actual participation by churches was minimal and yet, where it was undertaken, the response was impressive.

During a year of careful assessment of the first Radio Mission, North Kelvinside and its minister continued to be used in broadcasting including a notable Overseas Service for Good Friday. It was no surprise therefore when a second Radio Mission was to be mounted in 1952, Tom Allan was appointed the chief Missioner. This time there was a much wider willingness by churches and whole presbyteries to be involved. A selection of Scottish centres were chosen as being representative of the main types of Church situation found in Scotland. Tom was given the job, through a series of Thursday night broadcasts, of preparing listening groups for practical mission in their own area and showing how the Radio Mission could help. It was a vital role which, by its success, would be later seen to point to the next step in harnessing his gifts for the benefit of the whole Church.

During the Radio Mission proper he had heavy responsibilities; an evening Home Service on 'What happens when we preach', a theme well illustrated in his popular ministry in North Kelvinside. Also he had, on two successive Sundays in March, the 'People's Service', known to have one of the largest listening figures of any broadcast. Here once more the media were enabling the evangelist, providing a service for the people, an opportunity for all, in an inclusive way, to hear the Gospel, understand the call of God on life, and rejoice in the open access to forgiveness, faith and fulfilment. Tom Allan was liberated to do 'the work of an evangelist' to which he was so obviously called.

The assessment of this Radio Mission indicated that the climate for evangelism in Scotland was sunny and warm, and that very many people were ready to respond positively, with commitment and faith. The BBC leaders decided that bringing these two promising factors together was the job of the Churches and not of the BBC. Nevertheless initiatives of the Churches acting together were promised the cooperation and support of BBC religious broadcasting. And so the 'Tell Scotland' Movement in Evangelism was born.

3   The Man for the Movement – 'Tell Scotland'

Since the War the Churches of Europe had been growing towards a consensus about Mission and Evangelism. Many bold, imaginative and demanding experiments had been carried out, evaluated and written up, in France and Germany, Holland and England, by Catholic and Reformed Churches and leaders. The World Council of Churches had a very active Department of Evangelism. Tom Allan's work in Glasgow brought him an invitation to serve in that department. He quickly grasped the significance of the various experiments and grappled with the questions they raised for the theology of evangelism. His influential book *The Face of my Parish* competently deals with the flood of material from all these sources but then assesses them honestly and vigorously against the reality of experience in his Glasgow parish.

The book is an excellent source of understanding the consensus which was emerging and which can be summarised by reference to the three principles of the 'Tell Scotland' Movement.

1 Mission is not an occasional or sporadic activity, but a continuous engagement with the world at every level;

2 The agent of mission is the Church;

3 The place of the lay person is decisive.

You may say that it would be easy for most to sign up to these principles but, in the Scotland of the early 1950s, they had a context which led to consensus. The immediate aftermath of the Radio Mission was the favourable climate for the churches to set up the 'Tell Scotland' Movement. The Steering Group was formed by the Radio Missioners, plus the heads of Evangelism Committees of the Churches, to whom were added some leading 'Elder Statesmen'. It was an effective mix, meeting once a fortnight at BBC Edinburgh for nearly two years, before launching an ambitious plan. Early in the planning stage it became clear that the Movement needed a full-time national leader. Tom Allan was the obvious choice and he left his parish in the autumn of 1953 to take up the post of 'Field Organiser of Evangelism – Tell Scotland'.

We need to pause for a moment here to understand the enormous nature of the change that this appointment brought to Tom Allan's life. The deep bonds of parish minister with his people were severed; the sharply focused objective of his preaching was shifted; the intensive long-term pastoral work with those won for the Church by the ongoing mission was impossible; his home was no longer the magnet for an endless stream of needy people seeking guidance; nor was it invaded every Saturday night by a veritable army of young people drawing from him teaching, challenge, inspiration, and genuine concern, all adding up to a relationship worthy to be called love, of the sort that reveals something of the love of God.

The new work was equally demanding – but different. Scotland was now his parish and he travelled it tirelessly, from top to bottom, and side to side. It was meeting ministers, addressing presbyteries, preaching in churches, teaching lay groups, challenging elders, all with the objective of preparing the Churches for the task of mission, a job he had been doing before – but now full-time. Yet every week increased the distance between the Organiser of Evangelism, and the active evangelist umbilically connected to people and parish.

Stated sharply like that is to ignore some of the logic of the situation. North Kelvinside parish developed on the basis of 'unilateral' plans and decisions of the parish minister and the parish church. But working with the BBC meant 'involvement' in the ecumenical dimension – with the voluntary opt out of the Roman Catholic Church. This was a whole new level of negotiation and co-operation, entered into more willingly by the Churches, because of the relationship with the media, than was possible at area or parish level. Again the Scotland-wide Movement had to cope with the theological diversity about Mission and Evangelism. George MacLeod's challenge that the Movement should be called 'Serve Scotland' not 'Tell Scotland' was an indicator. Also Ralph Morton's pamphlet 'Evangelism in Scotland Today' saw only rudimentary beginnings in the new directions for evangelism taken by 'Tell Scotland' and the missions which preceded it. In a quotation especially relevant because of what happened next he wrote, 'The day of the professional evangelist is past at least when he stood apart as the exponent of the faith to men. It is only through personal contact that men outside will be won. The members of the congregation are the agents of Mission. And that means a great change in the training and the life of Church members.'

Now Tom Allan not only agreed with that as wording, but had hammered it out in practice by the creation and sustaining of the Congregational Group in North Kelvinside. Willingly therefore he became for 'Tell Scotland' an enabler for evangelism, persuading ministers and members towards new priorities; assisting the emergence of lay groups on the basis of the three 'Tell Scotland' principles. At one point there were over 800 such groups struggling to integrate the Gospel into their daily living. Tom was driven by the vision, the all-inclusive vision, of nurturing the consensus Scotland-wide. It was enormously successful, but never easy. The ecumenical and theological questions were contained within the consensus, but only just and not for long.

The 'Tell Scotland' Movement had launched a well-planned three-year programme of mission. A year of preparation, planning and publications; a year of training the lay people of the churches by prayer, bible-study and practice in the congregational groups; and a year for the outreach by visitation, house groups, vocational cells, witness teams, open-air meetings, personal counselling and appropriate action in care and service. Of course, in keeping with the basic principles, the third year was meant to be but the beginning that would initiate the long-term engagement of a truly missionary parish. The plan was good. Indeed it was fundamental then and is fundamental now. But things changed with the arrival of Billy Graham and Mass Evangelism.

The relationship of Tom Allan, 'Tell Scotland' and Billy Graham needs careful examination. News of the 'Billy Graham' Crusades had crossed the Atlantic for years before the invitation to London by the Evangelical Alliance in spring 1954. The meetings were held in the Harringay Arena and the very professional publicity and administration, the thorough preparation, the reputation of the successful evangelist, brought overflowing crowds and, most impressive of all, thousands of converts, most of them young people. When the Crusade climaxed with 120,000 in Wembley Stadium after a tour of venues outside London, the clamour to have him in Scotland was reaching a crescendo.

So right in the middle of Tell Scotland's long-term strategy for evangelism with its emphasis on the local church and the lay folk as the evangelists, the Movement was faced with the urgent questions raised by the imminent arrival of Billy Graham. The immediate result was to shatter the consensus in the 'Tell Scotland' Steering Committee. The question came to the committee in a form requiring an urgent decision. Ronnie Falconer writes, 'There was no doubt at all that Billy Graham was to be invited to Scotland. By whom? A group of conservative evangelicals – or the churches? We agonised. Tom was the deciding factor. He went to London to sample Graham's Wembley Crusade. He came back, strangely moved, saying he believed we must invite Graham under Tell Scotland. We were hopelessly divided; yet unwilling to throw overboard such a devoted and charismatic brother as Tom. We held him in deep affection and respect; in the end we closed our ranks and went with him. Tell Scotland invited Billy Graham to carry out his All Scotland Crusade under its auspices. He agreed.'

Understanding Tom Allan's response to his Wembley visit involves us in a look back to North Kelvinside Church and before. It was Tom's bible-centred, evangelistic preaching and practice, albeit expressed from a Scottish Presbyterian base, and focused in a parish setting, which had called out 'the Congregational Group' which he believed was so central to long-term effective evangelism. In his travels for 'Tell Scotland' Tom was often confronted with the question 'How would this group of highly motivated committed laymen emerge in a congregation?' Remembering his own experience in North Kelvinside, he could see that if a local congregation could add to its own resources by using a gifted evangelist, then the membership of such a group to carry on the work when the Crusade was over, would be enhanced in numbers and in quality.

However two influences in Crusade evangelism seemed set to hinder this idealistic outcome. First there was no note struck in the 'simplistic certainties of Graham's teaching' which aimed to inspire Christian disciples to shoulder the awesome tasks of applying their faith to everyday life and work. This Christianity did not have Bonhoeffer's 'Cost of Discipleship' written into it as the only way in which the non-Christian world would notice, be influenced and convert. Secondly the 'do-it-yourself evangelism of inarticulate Church members was stopped in its tracks by the slick professionalism of the Graham Organisation.' Certainly that did happen, and certainly the quality of that organisation should be noted.

The alliance with 'Tell Scotland' and the official support of all mainline protestant Churches that went with it, did much for the All Scotland Crusade. It brought active participation and group attendance at meetings on a scale and comprehensive area coverage never known in Scotland before. It meant that the BBC gave open access to broadcasting, particularly on Good Friday and from Hampden Park later, but also special studio services and series with Billy Graham. It insured maximum co-operation and careful local preparation for a week of Scotland-wide land-line 'Relays' from the Kelvin Hall which brought the Crusade within reach of every Scot wherever they lived.

So, what did the Crusade do for 'Tell Scotland?' Assessments made with hindsight much later are very negative. Ronnie Falconer writes in 1978, 'However much many of us in Tell Scotland did not like the technique, modern Pop Festivals have made us modify our views on Mass Evangelism. Yet our objections to the Crusade remained. The content of Billy's message was not really in touch with our modern society. It would have been superb in 1855 instead of 1955. Strategically it encouraged those ministers and groups who had found the 'Tell Scotland' principle of the Creative Minority difficult, to breathe sighs of relief and say, 'Leave it all to Graham!' Thus we lost an impetus which was never recovered. More critically, Tom Allan our leader and inspirer followed Graham's ways and soon left us. None of those who succeeded him had his personal charisma, however hard they tried.'

Also, in an introduction to a reprint of Tom Allan's book *The Face of my Parish*, written in 1984, Professor James White wrote about the Crusade: 'When the tumult and the shouting died, and the figures were analysed, it was seen that Graham had not been an evangelist but an old fashioned revivalist. His impact on those outwith the Church was minimal; the Tell Scotland Movement never recovered from this colossal diversion.'

Contrast what Tom Allan wrote just after the Crusade. 'The Scottish Crusade provided an immense stimulus to the second phase of the Tell Scotland Movement. From every part of the country, reports have come of an entirely new response by the laity to the demands of the Movement. In hundreds of Churches throughout the land there are now Groups of lay people ready for the next step.'

In spite of the time gap between these radically opposed views, they call for explanation.. Only the story of his ministry in St George's Tron alongside the ancillary opportunities that it opened up, will provide the answers we need and at the same time pose the questions for the Church today that we may learn from them.

Before we leave Tom Allan's short period as Field Organiser of the 'Tell Scotland' Movement we should note, in a very general way, that the Crusade, and Tom Allan's subsequent departure did leave the Movement 'hopelessly divided' not only at the level of the Executive Committee, but also throughout the country. Scotland did see 'the Church fragmented as never before.' Ecumenism took centre stage, with the belief that the visible unity of Churches and their structures must precede any advance in its effective mission. The concept of 'Service' with 'Justice and Peace' as its objectives was advocated as the priority, and not the reputedly rather selfish 'survival' aim of membership of the Church or personal faith in the Gospel. The balance of Tom Allan's ministry, from its new city centre base, challenged these shifts in emphasis.

4   The Man for the City

The immediately noticeable characteristic of Tom Allan's move to St George's-Tron Church in central Glasgow was a dramatic change of role. Overnight he ceased to be an 'Organiser of Evangelism' and became once more an 'Evangelist'. Of course there is some cross over in the roles, but the essential difference needs to be clearly stated. In the Church of Scotland a 'call' is to a 'Congregation and Parish'. Of course this means ministering to the members. But it also means minister and members together serving the parish. The concept of the parish ensures that the minister is called to be an evangelist. The task is not only to baptise and nurture, but to call into confirmation. And more - to exercise a gift of communication and rapport with those outside the network of 'baptism, nurture, confirmation' so that they may really hear the Gospel and respond. And more yet - to use that same gift so that when others, perhaps by friendship or quality lifestyle have sufficiently attracted 'neighbours' to enquire about the faith, they may offer them, through the evangelist, a spiritually powerful encounter with the Gospel, to grip the mind, stir the conscience, reveal the choices and plead for the sake of the love of God to 'choose life'.

Tom was convinced from Easter in Reims that nothing in the world was more important than 'salvation in Jesus Christ'. He knew that 'salvation' was revealed by the astonishing immediacy of our involvement in the death of Christ on the cross – 'were you there?'; and that the liberating assurance of the forgiveness of sins and the love of God was received only at the same place and from the same source. Therefore proclaiming that Gospel was his calling and his lifework – the work of an evangelist.

The structure of the Church of Scotland is determined by the 'Articles Declaratory of the Constitution of the Church of Scotland in Matters Spiritual', that 'As a national Church representative of the Christian Faith and the Scottish People it acknowledges its distinctive call and duty to bring the ordinances of religion to the people in every parish of Scotland through a territorial ministry.'

Therefore in the Church of Scotland the only place for the 'Evangelist', as above defined, is in the Parish Ministry. Of course it is immediately said that every Parish Minister is an evangelist – wonderfully true in theory! But just as intellectual powers, pastoral skills, administration prowess, teaching ability, personal charisma and other gifts are spread in a very uneven way, so are the gifts of ministers for evangelism. How odd of God to arrange it in that 'unfair' way! Why give Tom Allan such natural excellence in golf, billiards, table tennis and every other sport using a moving ball, when only golf tried to correct 'the injustice of God' by giving opponents a 'handicap?'

From time to time in the course of the life of the Church someone emerges with a very special gift, often fully recognised only in retrospect. At best the Church has to resort to *ad hoc* arrangements to try to liberate these gifts for the benefit of the people and the good of the Church. As we follow Tom Allan with his extraordinary gifts into St George's-Tron we can see there a clear example of the way these circumstances evolved in a Scottish setting.

The city Churches and especially the city-centre Churches were being cited at this time as prime examples of the complete breakdown of the parish system and the consequent necessity for a total restructuring of the Church. Tom Allan's vision was that the principles and practice of the Missionary Parish as hammered out in North Kelvinside, were immediately applicable to St George's-Tron in the city centre as soon as the obvious characteristics of the city parish were identified and responded to appropriately.

Tom Allan had a meteoric entry to his new parish. Of course, he was not starting from scratch. He came with the enormous success of North Kelvinside behind him; the nation-wide reputation of his BBC broadcasts; his recognised book *The Face of my Parish*; the leadership he had provided for evangelism via Seaside Missions, United Christian Witness, and Monthly Rallies for Youth; the energetic and inspiring promotion of the 'Tell Scotland' Movement by journeys all over Scotland; his chairmanship of the All-Scotland Crusade; plus the opportunity and burden which all sections wanted to lay on his shoulders in the immediate aftermath of enthusiasm following the Crusade.

The first sign that he was 'trailing clouds of glory' into the new situation was the explosion of the Saturday night Youth Rallies. Started in September 1955, by December the Rallies were causing an accommodation problem. They were now 'admission by ticket only' and Relay Centres were set up in neighbouring large Churches. By April the following year five Churches were involved and in May and June nearly 5,000 people attended. Of course the follow through of the Crusade accounted for a great deal. But it is wrong to describe it as 'following Graham's ways'. Along with a group of ministers, mainly associated with Seaside Missions in the summer, these Rallies had been going and growing in North Kelvinside since September 1949. St George's-Tron gave them a new home where they continued throughout Tom Allan's ministry and until a new minister was appointed. This was effective evangelism, not sporadic or short term but sustained, accountable, tested and appreciated. Many congregations and individuals used these Rallies as an added dimension of their own work. They could bring their friends and contacts here to the evangelist and back for the nurture of the local congregations.

If the Rallies were the first sign, they were very quickly followed by the outline structure that was to serve for the whole ministry. Writing to the congregation in April 1956 Tom Allan quoted a Glasgow business man's complaint that St George's-Tron Church was 'holding up the business life of the city'. So be it – Tom suggested – the function of a parish Church at the commercial heart of the city is to guide, inspire and challenge that city's life with the unchanging message of the grace of God in Jesus Christ. He identified –
1 4,000 residents, promising shortly a visit from the Church with an invitation;
2 Half a million daily workers in the Parish, asking the question, 'What can we do in the light of the much publicised opinion that the focus for life today is not where people live, but where they work?

3 Evenings and weekends of leisure when Glaswegians and visitors crowd into the City centre. How would they find some connection, some relevant input to their lives from the Parish Church?

He promised no conventional ministry. Yet at the same time, that winter had been spent getting to know his members. The Sunday Morning Service had been established as 'the family' at worship with a new creche in the belfry. Here, with preaching, prayer and sacraments, were the all-sufficient resources for the daunting tasks of a Missionary Parish and for the deepest life-needs of the people. Soon the successful structure at North Kelvinside was put in place in adapted form in St George's-Tron. The vital role of the prayer meeting was emphasised, the Evening Service was developing as less formal, more evangelistic, widening out to include many visitors, attracting the attention of casual 'passers-by', and rapidly growing in attendances. After the Service a meeting for youth in the hall was becoming a magnet for students, nurses and other 'away-from-home' young people, as well as the youth of the congregation.

A crucial sign of the basic continuity of this ministry was established within fourteen months. He set up, for the whole Glasgow area, the 'Tell Scotland' School of Evangelism. Several distinguished speakers shared with him in this venture. It was the start of two strands to his new ministry which had been well illustrated in the past. First, the call to those in the congregation to study and train for witness and service. Second, to assist in the calling out of a wider 'Task Force' from the area around, that is the city and beyond, who would share the same objectives and pursue them both locally and co-operatively.

This was no *prima donna* evangelist blinkered into believing that he could do it all himself. He really believed that the Church was the agent of mission. He really did believe that the role of the evangelist and the vital place of the lay person do not constitute a divisive either/or for the Church. On the contrary, like all spiritual gifts, whether specialist to a few, widespread but uneven to many more, or universal to faith, they are given 'to prepare all God's people for the work of Christian service, in order to build up the body of Christ'. (Ephesians 4 v.12)

'The Church in the heart of the city with the city at its heart' was a motto adopted by St George's-Tron in all its publications. One of Tom Allan's early sermons gave the members of the congregation a clue to what their adopted motto would involve. Preaching from the parable of the 'Great Supper' he emphasised the Master's command, 'Hurry out to the streets and alleys of the town, and bring back the poor, the crippled, the blind, and the lame... so that my house will be full.' By the end of the ministry the motto was no longer a form of words which the Church had chosen, but an experience which the city had shared, and a publicly acknowledged fact which culminated in the award to Tom Allan from the City of Glasgow of the St Mungo Prize.

The involvement of the members of the congregation, the Group who willingly responded to the call to mission, started in a relatively low gear. The young people, many of them students, carried out the first friendship visit to the residents of the parish.

Top gear in the growing outreach to the city was reached with the Glasgow Central Churches Campaign. Tom's leadership brought together ministers and members of Presbyterian, Congregational, Methodist and Baptist Churches from the City Centre for an evangelistic and rehabilitation campaign. As Tom explained to his people, 'Round the all-night coffee stalls, pubs and cafes, where thousands spend their leisure, are gathered some of the greatest social problems of Glasgow.' A company director commented, 'It was amazing to see Christians from eight central Churches going out day and night to the homes, offices, pubs, clubs and coffee stalls, impelled by the compassion of Christ.' Tom himself led this 'Rescue Work' from the front, pleading with men and women at the coffee stalls till 3am in the early morning; creating an ambience of encouragement and friendliness for the many broken, hopeless, despairing, people who crowded into the Elgin Street Church Hall, open all night. 'He was truly Christ's gifted and winsome evangelist' was the verdict of his fellow ministers.

Did this sort of approach work? Two things happened immediately for St George's-Tron. People came from the streets to the Sunday Services, from sin to salvation, from fear to faith, from despair to destiny, from wreck to redemption. Later televised services show that the 'Master's house was filled' and the people from the streets and lanes of the city were there. The second thing that happened was that the lay workers realised that the complex network of circumstances, relationships, birth, intelligence and health which combined so inexorably to crush people, was not going to easily yield to the first forays of the Church seeking to apply the resources of the Gospel. Now they would learn to identify with the realism of their leader in Tom Allan's oft repeated cry of anguish and frustration, 'What can we do for these people?' He knew that the answer could not be some extension of the Rallies and Campaigns. The flickering candle of new faith and hope must not be left to be extinguished by the flood of sordid circumstances. A rehabilitation centre, with living accommodation attached was necessary to give that candle flame a chance.

Inspiring and co-operating with the Social Service Committee of the Church of Scotland opened up an exciting possibility. The Committee had premises in central Glasgow. Given some alterations and re-staffing one location could be a counselling and rehabilitation centre for women and girls with cubicles for 'overnight'. A second location could provide a rehabilitation hostel for women who needed guidance and direction over a period of time. This was great news, but what about money? Right away St George's-Tron launched a dual purpose scheme which once again shows the refusal to separate Church work into separate compartments. They set a target of £20,000, £10,000 would be used to re-equip the Church buildings for their growing evangelistic task and £10,000 would be a major contribution towards the costs of the social rehabilitation work. They achieved it - no small target in the late '50s. A great deal of the rest of the necessary capital costs were raised with help from many of the wide contacts and support that Tom Allan now had throughout the city and beyond.

Now that the professional resources were in place, and local authority, as well as many different social action organisations were using them, it would have been so easy to cut the umbilical cord connecting the evangelical mission of the Church to the long-term work of rehabilitation and integration. No, with Tom Allan's leadership, lay volunteers from the Church matured in the service they gave to the rehabilitation centre – making first contacts, befriending and encouraging, and sharing faith naturally. At last, a more substantial structure was in place for immediate response to blatant city centre social problems but they would work well only if the Church continued to ask the question, 'What can we do for these people?'

Just as Jesus' works of healing and reconciliation could not be hidden, so St George's-Tron and the name of Tom Allan became a unified 'Help' symbol for all in need in the city. Now a steady stream of desperate humanity swelled to a flood tide, threatening but never managing to engulf him. Queues would form after Sunday evening services and Saturday night Rallies to see him and often, when the situation was identified, would be passed on to volunteer workers to begin the necessary long-term friendship and follow-up. Tom Allan's social work never stopped short of the full compulsion and compassion of Christ's love. The goal was never simply enough bread to live, a roof over the head or a return to bodily health; but always these things as a first expression of the truth of Christ's transforming love and liberating pardon. So his evangelistic work was also his social work and vice versa.

The City's 'workers' were not forgotten. Vital rehabilitation work was so notable and important that there was some danger of it obscuring other developments. Communicating with 'the workers' commuting daily into the city took a stride forward after the contacts made by the Central Churches Campaign. That outreach was remarkably comprehensive, visiting the work places by careful arrangement and often early in the morning. The result was a volume of good will and good relationships that allowed for a variety of long-term contacts and facilities being developed. Some Christian 'cell-groups' were established where lay leadership evolved in a natural and acceptable way. An expressed need was met by the 'Worship before Work' short services provided early, every weekday. Conduct of these were shared between Tom and his assistants and also involved many guests from all denominations. Attendance and appreciation was consistent and encouraging while ebbing and swelling a bit in tune with the 'seasons' of the Christian year.

Experience with special seasons of 'Lunch-hour Services' led to them becoming a regular and very popular feature of city life. Holy Week, culminating on Good Friday, and 'Towards Christmas' building up to the festive break were quickly established. But experiments in other series like the innovative 'Two Men Open the Bible' when Tom Allan and a guest would talk through a biblical theme also brought a response from the city workers and visitors.

A particularly large 'workplace', the evolving Strathclyde University, forged a chaplaincy link with Tom Allan and St George's-Tron. Again he involved his assistants, some students and lay people in ways which formed important and fruitful links and communication.

A clear symbol of it all was the 'Open Church'. Daily from 8.30am to 5pm any one could go into 'the Church in the heart of the City' and find the quiet of the place of worship, to meditate, to pray and to rest in the Lord.

Tom combined a 'Ministry by the Media' alongside his other commitments. His first class Honours English was no barrier to his ability to adapt his 'Church speak' to the very different style of communication demanded by a weekly article for the Glasgow Evening Citizen. He gave a measured, thoughtful response to the advice of a seasoned journalist who asked, 'How would you put across your message to the man waiting at the Bridgeton Cross bus stop going to "the dogs" at Shawfield? Could you make him miss his bus?' 'I'll remember that chap at the bus stop,' he said.

Tom Allan valued the weekly Saturday article in the very popular 'Citizen' newspaper. It was an indirect extension of his work as an evangelist reaching thousands with no other contact with the Gospel or the Church. But he was in there on merit. His human interest 'stories' gleaned from personal encounters and his natural 'news sense' soon caught the readers' attention and the popularity of the articles was not lost on the 'Citizen' editors.

This entry into journalism had its own pressures. He would be asked, at the last minute, for a fresh article because of an emerging public interest 'story'. As 'The Citizen' explained, 'Within a few hours he would telephone the required copy.. Or he would come into the office, sit at a desk and write 1,000 words, straight off.'

Another peak was reached when 'The Citizen' sent Tom Allan in turn to Russia, the Holy Land, and to Rome, and commissioned a series of articles, a comment and assessment of each visit. They were a great success. Vivid observations of detail, attention-riveting human interest asides, accompanied by incisive analysis of the key interests raised by these locations, were all related to the foundation of faith on which he stood. This was his gift of communication at its best. No wonder when, years later, life was thrown into confusion by sudden illness, one possible alternative to the hectic life of St George's-Tron suggested to Tom Allan, was the editorship of a Christian newspaper. He had all the experience and certainly the gifts to do it brilliantly.

The other medium of broadcasting was equally important. Two things were happening there. First, radio was receding somewhat before the onslaught of television. Also the relationship forged at North Kelvinside and through the 'Tell Scotland' movement had changed following his appointment to St George's'Tron.

1961 was an important year... The BBC came to Tom Allan and St George's-Tron for 'Meeting Point at a City Centre'. The film followed the now familiar features of Tom Allan's City Centre work and achieved the difficult task of capturing on celluloid the elusive passion, personality and power of the preacher and the reality and scope of his involvement along with his people, in the throbbing varied life of the great city of Glasgow. It was an acclaimed production, shown in conference in Europe later as an example of the achievements of Scottish Religious Broadcasting.

Although Tom Allan suffered a heart attack in December 1961 he was able, after a year of careful recovery and on advice, to resume broadcasting along with all his other work. The result was an immediate flowering of his ministry and a widening of its reach. Again Easter was a focal point when in 1963 both Morning Service and Evening 'Songs of Praise' were televised from St George's-Tron. The national response to these services confirmed that Tom Allan had reached a new high in television communication.

There seemed no end to the variety and excellence of Tom Allan's output to the media. But one controlling factor should be noted – it was always part of his ministry, always directly connected to his calling as an evangelist, always pointing beyond himself, and his impressive gifts, to his Lord and his God.

How typical that the same year should see a quite contrasting type of programme. Challenging news about the harmful effects of smoking was beginning to escalate and Tom, a very heavy smoker, decided not only to stop himself but to ask others who wanted to join him. From the congregation at first, and then from others encouraged by doctors and social organisations a Group, an anti-smoking clinic, was formed.

It was publicly reported in the newspapers and the BBC decided to make a television programme about it. For Tom himself, it had all the agony of withdrawal from an addiction which was also true for many in the group. All aids to beat the habit were welcome. Medical information was given; money savings were emphasised ("Like my new suit? – fag money" cracked one Sunday worshipper;) mutual encouragement was fundamental; but for Tom the power behind it was spiritual. He talked, prayed and acted out himself the faith and its promises, passionately throwing himself and his friends, whether believers or not, on to the resources and assurances of Almighty God. Most of them, Tom included, made it then, and permanently. 'The Clinic' produced intimate and honest television revealing again that Tom Allan drew no dividing line between the Gospel preached, and sung, on Easter Sunday and the Gospel applied in a very practical situation to the daily lives of people, himself included.

A former Moderator of the Church of Scotland, Dr Sandy McDonald, captures the essence of it with a reference to a consultant physician dealing with people with lung trouble, who said, 'This guy, Tom Allan, has something that none of the rest of us have', and Sandy explains that this was not said from a religious standpoint. The man recognised Tom's passion to help people - in this case, those who were addicted to cigarettes, and it gave the doctor a new 'in' to the 'man of the cloth.' The 'something special' that Tom Allan had was the ability to build bridges, to be a link person, literally 'across the board'.

Is not this 'bridge building' ability, this function as a living 'link person', the very essence of the definition of an evangelist? It was recognisable right from the start of Tom's ministry. It was just after the war, when Tom was emerging from his final year of study, that he first climbed into a pulpit to preach. That very day he began his work as a mass evangelist. Of course we have to pay special attention here to definition.

Yes, the term 'Mass Evangelism' is loaded with American style overtones that have taken a deserved battering because of unfortunate practitioners in the USA. Nevertheless to understand Tom Allan we must establish the continuity and the integrity of all that developed from that earliest beginning.

Dr Ian Doyle in a timely article in 'Life and Work' (1986) remembers that first important preaching occasion for Tom. A student team under the Revd D.P. Thomson was conducting a post-war campaign in the Presbytery of Melrose. Tom had been impressive at some of the midweek meetings and both Ian and Tom were asked to preach at successive Sunday evening Rallies. Ian writes, 'Tom was nervous. I can remember still the awed hesitancy in his voice as he said to me, "Fancy me being asked to preach tonight." But D.P., as so often, had judged wisely. The congregation got rather more of Eliot's *The Waste Land* than they were prepared for! But the gift of being in contact with the audience was already there, the broad smile, the amusing story, the directness of appeal, that were to be so typical of later years.'

Facing nearly a thousand people in Selkirk Parish Church, with that awe and reverence for preaching which he never lost, revealing already that directness of appeal, was not this Tom Allan - mass evangelist in embryo? Every Sunday in the Church of Scotland a standard division of the worship service has –

1 Approach to God
2 The Word of God
3 Response to the Word of God
4 Blessing from God.

Any congregation with numbers too big for small group dynamics, and which follows this standard division of the service, is practising mass evangelism.

A different and important way in which the 'Mass Evangelist' is separated from the regular 'Parish Minister' is in the mysterious distribution of spiritual gifts as St Paul describes them. It is a matter of demonstrable fact in the history of the Church that, as in other spiritual gifts, some Christian leaders and preachers are endowed with gifts and spiritual power which combine to make them outstanding in the work of evangelism. This means that they are 'bridge builders' enabling crossings and contacts from unbelief to faith, from scepticism to searching, from doubt to discipleship. These are the very qualities that emerged early in Tom Allan. We have already traced them in the account of his ministry in North Kelvinside. But there remain other strands to explore.

We must register his successful practice of 'Mass Evangelism' in the Seaside Mission Work. How else could you describe the crowds that gathered to hear him on the low green at Ayr; the closing of the large putting greens at Girvan because he was preaching the Gospel there; or the 6,000 gathered on the tiered promenade at Aberdeen beach and broadcast on television.

Tom was adamant that this so-called 'Mass Evangelism', preaching for the response of faith, was not in conflict with the 'Tell Scotland' principle regarding the central place of the laity in evangelism. On the contrary, he saw these two tasks belonging essentially together, complementing each the other.

As Tom said in a broadcast, 'Some fire has to be kindled before the Tell Scotland Movement itself becomes incandescent. Something has to happen to the Church and the souls of its people. And it seems to me that it will come by three ways – not by one of them separately, for they cannot be separated. And not by a single journey along these three ways, but by a constant walking in them.'

First, the way of prayer for the people of Scotland by every congregation. Second, the way of practice, because the best preparation for mission is the work of mission itself. Third, is the way of preaching, 'Mass Evangelism,' if you like. Preaching for a verdict has always been a part of the Church's ministry. It is to be recognised as part of the Church's divine commission.

A flood of invitations now came asking Tom to undertake 'Mini-Crusades' in Scotland and some 'Maxi-Crusades' in Canada - all very fruitful. David McNee, then a distinguished police inspector in Glasgow and later head of the Metropolitan Police in London, partnered Tom as solo singer for all of these Missions.

Such success as an evangelist was bound to issue in invitations outside of Scotland and it did, particularly to Canada. His first city-wide Mission was in Hamilton, Ontario. It was well organised and very demanding. Stan Boulter writes from Hamilton, 'Tom Allan was known only in name but before the mission ended he was acclaimed as the greatest and most beloved evangelist ever to visit this country.' Strong words indeed, but here is a different quote, 'Mr Allan's evangelism was grounded in a sound biblical theology. It was rooted in the Christian hope rather than in morbid fear. The Resurrection was pivotal to his preaching. He positively affirmed the primacy and centrality of Jesus Christ as Saviour and Lord.'

Two other major Canada Missions followed in Calgary and Halifax. The results and the assessments were reported in the same glowing terms. Can we understand the pressure, the agonising decision-making, the searching for God's guidance that would confront Tom Allan as he was asked to give up being Parish Minister/Evangelist of the Church of Scotland and respond to a variety of invitations from America and Canada to be a full-time mass evangelist? Only those without imagination and who would never face like dilemmas would dismiss such a situation with trite guidance or solutions.

Professor J.S. Stewart speaks of 'Tom Allan's full-orbed ministry'. 'As a preacher his message glowed with evangelistic fervour, as he pointed his hearers to Calvary and the empty tomb; but there was also this, that all the time he was taking upon himself the burden of the plight of men, and involving himself sacrificially in all the conditions of their life'.

However it is true to Tom Allan's understanding of his calling, wonderfully true to his 'full-orbed ministry' that he centred his work in St George's-Tron, making his contribution to mass evangelism, yet realistically adhering to his honest conviction that this was but one part, and only one, of the Church's obedience. He knew that the Glasgow work force, the city tourists and leisure and pleasure seekers, the social outcasts and down-and-outs, could not be reached by mass evangelism working in isolation. He wrote, 'Is this technique in evangelism adequate by itself to fulfil our missionary obligation? What of the millions who have not been to a crusade? Have they to be by-passed, left to their fate? Is the Gospel only for those who will attend a religious meeting?'

The sweep of his City Centre ministry answers this question with a resounding 'No'. It illustrates the sacrificial and unrelenting efforts in teaching and training, practice and prayer, cells and services, libraries and lodging houses, coffee stalls and pub-crawls, all with one clear purpose - 'to hold up the life of Glasgow' and to challenge every part of its throbbing life with Jesus' proclamation 'The Kingdom of God has come'. This was a comprehensive effort to liberate and equip the whole Church to be the 'Agent of Mission' where it was set and lived – to be a 'living cell in the everlasting Church.'

5   The Message from the Man

Tom Allan died in September 1965, aged 49 years. Can there be a message for the new millennium from 35 years ago? Indeed there is. Tom would have said there is only one message and it is from the One whose coming started the millennium count – Jesus Christ. But there are particular aspects of that message which stand out as relevant and are well illustrated in the 'Tom Allan Story'. The first aspect comes at the basic level of **home and family life.**

Some observers have deduced that Tom Allan's amazing achievements in so many different directions must have had destructive consequences on his home and family life, which they think may purchase his success at an unacceptable cost to his family.

The first thing to say right away, to put the record straight, is that this was a co-operative effort. Jean and Tom Allan were in this together from day one and the verdict of all those who knew the inside of their home was that here was a truly Christian base, nurturing three very much loved and privileged children.

It must be said that the Manse in Clouston Street, North Kelvinside was not your average residence. Tom always believed in community or maybe communality and he and Jean shared their home with some of the idealism of these words very much in mind. Verses that were frequently expounded and explored in practical ways, were the final few of Acts Two. They give a picture of the early Church believers continually together in fellowship. They were sharing, eating, worshipping, and witnessing together with great joy. It is a wonder that Manse didn't develop elastic sides to cope with the variety of sharing, eating, learning, praying, worshipping and witnessing that went on within its walls.

Of course the Manse was right in the parish in close proximity to the Church. But it was not the usual emergency calls for pastoral services like funerals and weddings that made up its visitors. For one thing, most of the assistants were resident there for part of their time – some for a whole year. Then ministers' groups would arrive for planning, discussion, study of scripture or theology and to pray.. Later a working office had to be set up in the Manse with a resident secretary to cope with the demands of administration.

But that was by no means all. The Saturday invasion by young people has been mentioned. Add to that an ever-growing trail of needy people seeking Tom Allan. It was a working manse and a wonderful home.

The ample testimony of Andrew Moyes – rebellious teenager in North Kelvinside, who viewed himself as an unlikely candidate for the Ministry, but who later became assistant to Tom in St George's-Tron says it all, 'One thing we discovered, that it was impossible to know Tom Allan and not be challenged by Jesus Christ. For another thing we discovered what a Christian home could be like. Tom Allan was always a man with a great sense of "family", and my wife and I will be forever grateful for all we learned at "the Allans" of the place and influence of Christ in the family.'

But what of the life of the larger family, **the family of the local Church?** It has been argued that Tom Allan was driven by the dramatic incident of Easter at Reims and some turn that observation into a critical assessment of his work. They reckon that he really wanted all Christians to come to faith in the same dramatic way. They even suggest he was saying, as some 'evangelicals' do, that the ability to relate a time and place for a dramatic conversion are a prerequisite to being a real, true, motivated, serving Christian. They go on to criticise Tom's 'priority for evangelism' and the important place he gave to 'preaching for a verdict'. Thus they attempt to press his work into a narrow corner making it only marginally relevant to the mainstream work of the Church – especially its 'nurture' programme.

Three counts argue against this distortion. First, Tom always gratefully acknowledged the nurture and growth in faith given in his own home and local Church and community. Second, we have his written statements on the subject making it clear that he knew very well that the way to faith has many varied and flexible patterns, almost as many as individual believers. He insists that how someone travels to being a Christian is not so important. What is vital is the self-conscious, powerfully motivating conviction that Jesus Christ is Lord and Saviour. He saw his preaching as an evangelist providing opportunity for a personal encounter with the risen Lord, with the good news of the Gospel, issuing in affirmation, re-affirmation, fresh affirmations, or a new level of affirmation of faith.

Third, and perhaps most important, were his own actions related to this matter. In both his parishes Tom was very orthodox in the attention given to, and the emphasis placed on, the 'nurture' road to faith. Sunday Schools, Bible Classes, Youth Groups and Christian Youth Organisations were very important to him and were encouraged by him. One extraordinary statement of his held that 'the Minister should always be Superintendent of his own Sunday School', because nurture and education of the children, was too basic a responsibility of parish ministry to have it otherwise. And what minister would have 30-40, on occasion 50, young people in teens and early twenties 'invade' his home every Saturday night and sit down with them to listen, befriend, talk, share, and want to come back the next Saturday! A recent reunion of members of that group recalled it with joy, and a deep sense of privilege. This was a 'sowing and watering' ministry as well as 'reaping'. Here was a natural affection for children, a soaring inspiration for youth's dreams, a sacrificial open door to a Christian home, and an even more open heart to a warm, loving person.

Only a superficial judgement, essentially unaware of the facts, could box this ministry into any trivialising categories and certainly not a box marked 'single-track conversionism'.

However, in today's climate, when the nurture net has shrunk in size and in many places torn, when fresh faith and new members are going to come from a standing start or not at all, the Church will have to give the opportunity for 'the reaper'. The more 'nurture' and 'bridge building' that goes on the better. But the chance of the explosive encounter, the impassioned communication of the Gospel of a risen Lord and a contemporary crucified Saviour will have to be a regular and not a sporadic part of the Church's ministry.

The work of an evangelist is more urgent than ever. Will the Church search out and find the gift within its ranks, and, when it does, will it be able to maximise and liberate the gift, free of the trivial, weakening either/or arguments like 'nurture versus dramatic' when describing the way to faith?

Now that raises the question of **'New forms of ministry'** to meet the needs of today's Church.

Tom Allan had two parishes. However it would be true to say that in both he 'broke the mould' to some extent or rather he expanded any narrow concept of parish ministry. This was especially true of the City Centre Parish. He also, albeit for a short period, was appointed to a different form of ministry as combining a responsibility for Summer Missions with Field Organiser of 'Tell Scotland'.

Tom spoke of the Parish Ministry with deep affection. He saw it as one of the most privileged relationships possible with people. It is made uniquely available by being an established Church. In spite of changing times, the minister and the Church community still have an open opportunity to offer to the people the moral, spiritual counselling and comforting services of the Parish Church. North Kelvinside is really the story of, at first tentatively and then confidently delivering such service in the name of Christ. The result was warm and welcoming relationships, open homes and open hearts. The move from the parish to a new form of ministry was a wrench.

But the national Church, impelled by the discoveries of the media, recognised his special gifts and wanted to liberate them more widely for the benefit of the Church generally. The appointment, really aimed to kick-start the emerging embryo of the 'Tell Scotland' Movement, had to be given an existing 'cover', within the structures of the Home Mission Department of the Church. D.P. Thomson's responsibility for 'evangelism' was split and Tom was given the job of Seaside Mission Organiser along with Field Organiser of 'Tell Scotland'. This mechanism managed the essentials of a salary and a house. It was the only way of covering the essentials outside of the norm of Parish Ministry. It worked well in many ways and certainly achieved its main objectives, but it must be recognised that it was an *ad hoc* arrangement hurriedly put in place to meet the pressure of developing circumstances. It reveals the truth that the Church of Scotland does not have much flexibility to respond to 'other forms of ministry' especially when spiritual ministry gifts emerge which cannot be predicted, trained for, or related to qualifications like PhDs. Sometimes the Catholic or Anglican Churches can be judged more flexible because of the authority for direction of clergy given to the Bishop or Archbishop. These Churches have demonstrated this by appointing specialists in communication through the media of radio and television.

Other forms of ministry have already been pioneered as in 'chaplaincies' and 'community ministers' to name two which recognise 'pastoral' and 'bridge building' gifts. The post millennium Church will need more and different skills. There are difficulties to overcome of a structural and economic nature. But there are other dangerous downsides which need to be avoided and which are well illustrated in Tom Allan's appointment.

The gifts and insights which were so clearly demonstrated in the parish setting cannot always be readily transferred, practised and succeed out of the parish. The subtle nature of the relationships which flow and transfer easily from one level to another are not easily replicated. In a sense Tom Allan was suddenly bereft of all these relationships when he left the Parish – and he felt it.

The new structure, the new form of ministry was immediately in danger of not fulfilling its key purpose. The most important gift, that of an evangelist - creating the opportunity for the message to go where it had not been able to go before - was being sacrificed to another priority. The task now was the recruitment of lay groups so that they could become the evangelists where no preacher could penetrate.

Now this calling out of the laity was and is essential. But the creation, training and perfecting by practice of such a congregational group was passionate and patient work in a parish setting, backed by much prayer and sacrifice. The peripatetic ministry of a 'Field Organiser' could but pass on the principles, encourage the ministers and create a first base receptive attitude among the office-bearers and congregation. Useful work, but not quite the level and depth at which Tom Allan was used to working and which he craved as his calling.

This is not in the least designed to argue against 'new forms of ministry' - quite the opposite. Rather it is to illustrate the complexity of structuring these forms to maintain the basic building block of parish ministry.

More recently, a parish minister showed special abilities for evangelism. When he was asked to be one of the 'area organisers' for evangelism, he said he would only do it if he was allowed to maintain his links with the parish. It seems an impossible request. Yet with flexible structures for help in the parish, linked with activities outwith, it is one way worth exploring.

One thing is clear. Tom Allan found in the Parish Ministry, in city suburb and city centre, a *milieu* in which his calling from God and his ordination to the ministry of the Church were able to be expressed so effectively that the outflow is running strong to this day.

These issues, united with others, bring into sharp focus the main 'Message from the Man'. It could be legitimately described as 'The Priority of the Parish'. The fact that a Church of Scotland minister is ordained and inducted to a Congregation and **Parish** is illuminating. In keeping with God's view of the world, so for the minister of a Parish (a more or less manageable slice of the world) 'Everybody is in and nobody is left out, everybody matters and nobody is undervalued, everybody belongs and nobody is excluded or marginalised.' It is a simple corollary to say that every parish minister is therefore an evangelist. But more, it follows that every Congregation is an 'Agent of mission' along with the minister, as the 'Tell Scotland' Movement emphasised.

The clarity of this could be slightly clouded in Tom's case by the ever more obvious fact that he was also called to a **Specialist form of ministry – an evangelist with particular gifts**. Yet always for him the whole Church, every minister and every Congregation was called to the same priority. There is therefore no escaping the one central question raised by his ministry. Is evangelism the priority for the Church? Is the Church today obedient to the great commandment of Jesus repeated five times in the New Testament? The command to his followers is in each of the Gospels and reiterated in Acts in different forms. It is essentially 'Go into all the world and make disciples'.

All eighteen years of Tom Allan's short but intensive ministry give the priority to evangelism. Therefore that ministry raises the question sharply, 'Is evangelism the priority for the Church?'

What about the 'Ecumenical Imperative', so often quoting Jesus' prayer, 'May they be one, so that the world will believe,' seeming to give priority to the need for the unity of the Church? Without discussing the exegesis of Jesus' prayer in John 17 we must note Tom Allan's challenge remains. While he was much engaged in cooperation across the denominations, it was always in the cause of evangelism and never in search of a structure for unity. Witness the Glasgow Churches Campaign 1950, the Glasgow Central Churches Campaign, the Radio Mission, the 'Tell Scotland' Movement and even the All Scotland Crusade and perhaps most significantly the World Council of Churches Department of Evangelism.

No one can doubt that there has been a shift in today's Church. The pressures of pluralist societies, a multi-faith world, and a very powerful secularist influence, have blunted evangelism and encouraged ecumenism. The question remains, is it a right shift? Tom Allan's ministry is a vital part of the evidence for the Priority of Evangelism.

The same question arises, perhaps even more sharply, in the overseas work of the Church. It is not simply that our overseas personnel no longer go to a 'pioneer' situation but always to serve with a local Church now established. So often their work has to be carefully protected from any hint of involvement with evangelism perhaps because of the state authority but just as often because of the secondary place which the local Church now gives to evangelism. Again Tom Allan's ministry raises urgent questions. He wrote, 'Evangelism is something the Church ought to be doing *all the time*'. The greatest danger is 'allowing this kind of work to be done only by American evangelists or by sects outside the mainstream of the Christian tradition.'

The evidence these days from overseas is of burgeoning evangelism especially by 'independent' Churches, while at home priority is given to ecumenism by the 'traditional' Churches which may be driven as much by retreat and economics as by conviction. Also very striking, is the reaction of overseas ministers and Church workers coming to Scotland. They arrive with a great sense of reverence for, and inspiration from, the missionaries who brought the Faith to them and their people. They are often shocked to find the Churches here no longer give passionate priority to the sharing of that Gospel.

Again Tom Allan would be astonished at one current view that there is something 'non-Christian' about evangelism that aims to win new members! Such a drive is criticised as 'survivalism'. But if 'member' of the Church means a living part of the 'Body of Christ' then that's exactly what he was looking for.

How has the Church managed to confuse the 'Follow me' of Jesus with some reprehensible manipulation of people by extremist sects or indoctrination procedures of totalitarian religious or secular systems? The result has been to blunt the clear call of all scripture to convert, to turn from all others to the God and Father of our Lord Jesus Christ.

Tom Allan rejoiced that 800 new members joined North Kelvinside Church in five years. Of course, realist that he was, he understood that among them there was a great variety in the level of spiritual awareness that God had given to each individual. His challenge to the Church now, in a very different climate, is that one factor, among other important ones, responsible for the membership decline in the Church, is the fact that evangelism, the communication of the Gospel for the response of faith, is no longer the priority.

On a wider scale, where is the focus of the World Council of Churches today? While it has continued to pay homage to earlier leaders like Lesslie Newbigin, in practice its interest in mission has developed in ways alien to his thought, with the result that much of Bishop Newbigin's later writing had, as one of its aims, the recall of the WCC to a biblical view of mission.

Tom Allan was openly and honestly involved in seeking for insights and guidance from the WCC about the *milieu*, methods and goals of evangelism.

He read avidly and widely all that he could find on the subject. Often he wished that the theological reports might be less locked up in technical language. Wrestle with them he did, and his profound understanding of the present problems of evangelism were revealed by his book and by his interventions at the times of the meetings, when he quickly assumed great authority. But always he assessed the conclusions and their consequences, by reference to the practical realities in his parishes and parishes he visited throughout Scotland. His final non-negotiable reference point was always Easter at Reims.

Much closer to home, the same listening, learning, understanding and assessing, faced him in his whole ministry in Scotland. D.P. Thomson wrote, 'He showed the rare gift of being able to work with men of very different types and temperaments to his own and of different theological outlook also. I could not fail to admire the patience with which he grappled with the infinite variety of problems emerging month by month as the 'Tell Scotland' Movement developed.'

Tom Allan remained 'his own man' in the midst of all this. Along with other ministers at the time, he was determined to hold the middle ground, as it were, and turn neither to the right nor to the left in the direction of extreme positions. But without a doubt the focal point for him was the primacy of evangelism. Getting that right, not as a theory but as an all-embracing passion and life-driving power, put all else in place and perspective.

What is the focal point for today's Church? When he was dying, Tom Allan spoke of his experience of ministry as a balancing act. He said, 'I've been walking on a tightrope all my ministry, and there's people on both sides been trying to pull me off, and only in the power of the Holy Spirit can I stay on track. But that doesn't mean that I want to disown those on either side.'

The Church has lived for most of its history in more or less alien cultures. Its life-blood has flowed with its ability to share its faith by word and life. All who knew Tom Allan testify to the healthy, balanced insistence that every nerve, fibre and resource of the Church should be openly and joyfully directed to sharing the faith as a natural expression of what had been received. St Paul says, 'We are ruled by the love of Christ'. Worthy evangelism is a reflection of that love extended through the Church to people and parish.

In the end 'The Man is the Message' in a special sense. Tom was the warm, loving, vulnerable, human person that everybody wanted to be with. But he was a man with a passion. A master passion he expressed memorably:

> It is for this that we are called as Christians...
> that the world should look beyond us to Christ,
> seeing perhaps in us some fraction of His image.

We saw. We saw beyond, and were blest.